The Laws Of Medicine

LEGAL STRATEGY FOR GROWING HEALTHY BUSINESSES

David 'DJ' Holt

THE LAWS OF MEDICINE
Legal Strategy for Growing Healthy Businesses

Copyright © 2025 David Holt
All rights reserved.

ISBN: 978-1-964046-79-2

The information provided in this book is for informational purposes only and is not intended to be a source of advice or credit analysis with respect to the material presented. The information and/or documents contained in this book do not constitute legal or financial advice and should never be used without first consulting an insurance professional and/or a financial professional to determine what may be best for your individual needs.

The publisher and the author do not make any guarantee or other promise as to any results that may be obtained from using the content of this book. You should never make any investment decision without first consulting with your own financial advisor and conducting your own research and due diligence. To the maximum extent permitted by law, the publisher and the author disclaim any and all liability in the event any information, commentary, analysis, opinions, advice, and/or recommendations contained in this book prove to be inaccurate, incomplete, or unreliable or result in any investment or other losses.

Although the author and publisher have made every effort to ensure that the information in this book was correct at press time, the author and publisher do not assume and hereby disclaim any liability to any party for any loss, damage, or disruption caused by errors or omissions, whether such errors or omissions result from negligence, accident, or any other cause.

Content contained or made available through this book is not intended to and does not constitute legal advice or investment advice, and no attorney-client relationship is formed. The publisher and the author are providing this book and its contents on an "as is" basis. Your use of the information in this book is at your own risk.

Editing by Ryan Huber
Copyediting by Lori Price
Proofreading by Lucy Spencer
Text design and composition by Emily Fritz
Cover design by Casey Fritz

Introduction
Electroshock Therapy

It turns out, nearly dying from electrocution can bring clarity to your life.

Years ago, I bought this beautiful duplex in south Minneapolis, right by the lakes. I actually put an offer on it without ever seeing it. I was in California at the time with my (ex) partner and our son. The three of us were in California, staying in various Airbnbs during the COVID-19 pandemic. It was 2021, and we had been house hunting for a while.

We were in the process of separating, so we were looking for a duplex where she could live on the top level, I could live on the lower level, and our son could go in between. I'm the financially-minded partner, so I was doing most of the administrative work as we looked to buy a home.

I purchased the duplex, and we moved in. It was a really beautiful, turnkey, 1920s Tudor-style place. But there were these lights outside the front with an old, almost Gothic feel. One of them was always out. The other one wasn't structurally sound; everything about them seemed bad.

So a couple months after we closed, I decided to take on this little electrical project. I went down to the basement and turned off the power—to what I thought was both of the front lights. In a duplex, though, especially one with partial 1920s wiring, things aren't always intuitive.

The way they had wired it, one panel controlled one light. The other panel, which would normally control all the circuits in the upper unit, also controlled the second light. Kind of a unique setup. I'm not an electrician. I should have just shut off the power to the entire house, but I didn't want to turn off the refrigerator, microwave, and everything else in my ex's unit. And I thought I had turned off both lights.

I went out there with all my tools and gear. I changed out the first fixture with little issue. I was proud of myself. I removed the old light fixture, cut the wire, mounted the new fixture, glued it in, and went downstairs to test it. When I came back upstairs, it was working. Awesome! I was excited.

I think one reason I assumed the power was off on the second light was that when I did my test, it didn't come on. But now I think the bulb just wasn't working, or maybe a wire was loose. As I started on the second fixture, using the same process, I grabbed my wire cutter and cut the wire. Immediately, sparks flew.

Fortunately, it was a clean cut.

I dropped the wire cutter and thought, "Wait . . . is the power on? Or is it supposed to do that?" Then it hit me. I had just cut through a live wire. Why didn't I get electrocuted?

I went back downstairs and shut off the power to the entire unit. I checked the current—something I probably should have done at the start. But I wanted to "do it myself."

Then I said it out loud. "Holy crap! I just cut through a live wire." I was really jacked up. I didn't really know what to do, so I stopped the project for a few hours.

Later, I looked at the wire cutter. One of the blades had melted completely through. The metal was deformed, and the tool wasn't even that long. How that current didn't transfer to my body, I don't know. It felt like divine intervention.

I'm not a religious person. But that was a real wake-up call.

It was a warm, sunny summer day. It could have been my last. No one else was home. Not many neighbors were outside. I could have just laid there, electrocuted, with no one to help me.

I thought about my son, Milo. I had a vivid picture of him playing with Legos in his room. I could see him so clearly. What if I, his dad, had died that day?

That was a big wake-up call for me. I needed to be more present as a parent. I couldn't take needless risks, especially when I lacked expertise. And it wasn't just about electrical work. I began to reevaluate how I was treating my body, my mind, and my health. I brought a new attitude to life in general.

I thought about the new lights I had installed. They were extremely bright, and I had adjusted their motion sensors to the most sensitive setting. They would pick up people just walking by or even cars driving past. But I'd rather have them be more sensitive than less sensitive.

The new lights became a metaphor for the changes I wanted to make in my life: to be more intentional, to calibrate things, to renew my focus, to fully show up to the rest of the time I have.

As I reflected, I realized some things in my life needed serious tweaking. I always liked the idea of being the handyman. Starting a project excited me. I derived fulfillment from doing this project by myself. I had fixed some light fixtures in my house before. I had an engineering degree. I figured I was capable and thought, "I got this." But I had never done this type of project.

But I was a biomedical engineer—not an electrician. I had learned medical device design, not electrical wiring.

I also grew up in a frugal household. We would fix things ourselves. Our method was "just figure it out." Why pay $100 an hour for an electrician—or anyone—if you didn't really have to? The whole concept of hiring skilled labor was foreign to me. It was the way I grew up.

I always wanted to own the project. I wanted to make it my own, even if it was terrible. I see this with business owners all the time—people building their own websites, resisting SEO help, and clinging to the DIY mentality. I identify with that; I initially resisted a lot of the SEO website design for my own business. Ownership is important.

But it's not worth killing yourself for.

I could have researched more, consulted someone, or just watched a video from an electrician's YouTube channel. I needed expert help.

Now, things have changed. Years later, I'm almost on the opposite end of the DIY spectrum. I don't garden. I don't shovel snow. I don't do repairs. I rarely do my own cleaning. I've even hired an au pair.

I'm a highly skilled technician myself. People pay me well for my technical expertise. And I now pay others for their expertise. I respect their skills and the fine work they do. I also value my time. For the last few years, I've been buying back my time.

Buying back time is critical if you want your business to grow.

I completely understand why smart people insist on doing it themselves. If you've built something and you have some knowledge and background, why wouldn't you think, *I can handle this.* And sometimes you can.

But it only takes one time or one mistake to leave you dead in the water. Cut the wrong wire, and you're dead. Take the "do-it-yourself" approach to medical law, make one mistake, and your business is dead.

Even if you don't lose your license, any stain on your record can follow you forever. It's public. It's damaging. And it's difficult to come back from. Licensing boards can be as unforgiving as a live current.

They have no sympathy for your explanations. They don't care why you didn't hire an attorney or why you rammed something through. Their job is to protect the public and keep commerce moving. Their role is regulatory, not rehabilitative, and the system can be harsh.

This is especially true in places like Minnesota, California, and New York. State governments hold all the cards. If you ping their radar, they can shut you down—just like that—with all legal authority at their back.

And whether you think that's fair or not is irrelevant. When you got your license, you signed up to play by their rules. You may not agree with all the rules, but unless you change them in the legislature, you've got to play by those rules.

That's why the stakes are so high.

As I thought about what my funeral would have looked like—had I died that day—I realized how high the stakes are for my life. I had to admit I'd just been coasting. Life was pretty good. I made enough money. I had family and friends. I was physically fit. But there was plenty more in the tank, and why wasn't I using it?

I hadn't made a big impact yet. I hadn't helped as many businesses as I would have liked. I wasn't being intentional in my parenting or in any of my relationships. I wasn't really working on my physical or mental health or my spiritual life. I was just comfortable.

And it's easy to just stay comfortable. Easy to talk yourself out of the workout. Easy to settle for the status quo.

I had gotten comfortable from a business standpoint, too. I wasn't hiring the best book guy, the best marketing gal, or the best website support. I wasn't leveraging experts or building a real team.

But after that electrical scare, I changed.

I started asking for help—not just in business, but also in my personal life. I upped my therapy game. Joined a men's group. Got serious about my fitness with intense workouts five times a week.

I began investing in myself—intentionally and intensely—by learning from the best. I read the best books in every category, whether it was business, diet, organization, or leadership. I asked experts for resource recommendations. I hired a business coach and, later, a better one.

And it's changed everything for me.

Now, when there's an issue or project, my first gut instinct is, *Who can I hire to do this?*, not *How do I do this myself?*

My near-electrocution made all the difference. I learned the value of experts and the cost of inexperience. I learned the danger of wasting time and energy trying to go it alone in our lives and in our businesses.

That's what I now do for my clients. I help them avoid cutting the wrong wire. I help them grow strong, healthy businesses.

And that's why I wrote this book. If you're looking to grow your business, keep reading. These are the Laws of Medicine.

Chapter 1
The First Law of Business Health: Practice Perfect

I imagine you have some questions. After all, I did just tell you I almost electrocuted myself. So you may be wondering why you should trust anything I have to say—about law, medicine, or business. I wouldn't blame you for asking the question: "Who is this guy?" I think I can help with that question.

Who Is DJ Holt?
First and foremost, I am a person who has been formed by my *practices*, whether that's the practice of yoga, the practice of parenting, or the practice of law. Before that, it was the practice of learning about the medical system, figuring out whether I wanted to go into medicine, and working to become a medical engineer. These are the practices I've spent my adult life investing in. These practices have made me who I am.

Yoga

Over the last two years, I've hit the practice of hot yoga hard. But I built this intentional yoga practice on a broader, years-long habit of exercise and a healthy lifestyle.

I used to be an inconsistent workout person. I benefit from a pretty high metabolism, and when you're young, that helps you look good for a potential partner or someone you're trying to pursue.

I got into yoga a few years ago because of my ex. She was a yoga instructor and acupuncturist and knew a lot of yoga instructors.

So mostly through osmosis, I got involved in yoga. I liked both the meditation and the workout. It's why I landed on sculpting yoga. You spend five to seven minutes out of the sixty asking yourself, *"What's my intention?"* There's a brief meditation, and then boom. You're stretching, you're in, and then all of a sudden you're sweating. Weights are flying around, and you're getting more toned than with other forms of yoga.

I wanted a more intense experience. Yin yoga is great for the body, but I only do that occasionally to slow things down. With limited time, I want yoga to give me a "one-two-three punch": get rid of toxins through heat and sweat, do an actual workout including cardio and toning, and add in a bit of meditation—all in one hour a day, five times a week. This practice has changed my life.

Recently, I've also added weight training with a personal trainer, cold plunges, and sauna treatments. All this takes a real commitment to consistency, but the results speak for themselves. I have more energy, my brain is sharper, and I'm getting more toned each month.

Even more importantly, this has created structure and routine in my life. The discipline to work out, even when you don't want to, trains your brain. It builds resilience and self-control. Years ago, I would make excuses to wiggle out of things I didn't want to do. You can make excuses for anything. Now my mentality is "No excuses."

This change has helped my blood pressure, sleep, and expected lifespan. It also forced me to structure my business differently. I built my business around the things that are important to me: my son, Milo, and my overall health. Most people build a business first and then organize their life around it. Quality of life issues are secondary to the success of their business. I decided to do the reverse.

This is real prioritization. On a given day, I work out from four to five in the afternoon, then pick up Milo. I block that time off, even though it's during a normal workday. I've extended this principle to my team. I pay for my employees to work out. If they are contractors, they can bill me for an hour. I even pay for the time it takes for my employees to get there and back and for them to shift gears. My only criterion is that I want intensity, not just dog walking.

Why do I do this? Too many employees say, "I don't have time to work out." So I eliminate that excuse by giving them the paid time to do it.

Nearly 100 percent of our staff have taken me up on this offer. The benefits are huge—better brain health, better productivity, better work relationships, better work experience. It's also incredible for employee retention.

I don't know why most companies fail to do this. People won't leave jobs that allow them to prioritize their health and quality of life.

All this came, in one way or another, from my yoga practice.

Medicine?

When you're a kid, you feel like you have to pick the right career. Unfortunately, no one knows what the hell they want to be when they're sixteen.

I considered medicine as a career. It was a kind of journey for me. The practice of investigating medicine as a potential career path taught me a lot about our medical and health care systems.

My dad was a finance director at 3M. As an accountant, he was a practical guy. When I was approaching eighteen, we had the standard career conversation, and of course, medicine came up. But I'm not good with blood or needles. I *was* interested, though. Maybe I could come at it from an engineering perspective. I could envision making the device that goes into the body, but not being the guy who puts it there. So I ruled out becoming a doctor.

I tried. I shadowed a doctor. I remember sitting in the office with an elderly couple, listening as the doctor talked with them. It was depressing. They were on a bunch of medications, and then he removed some sort of skin growth. I thought, *This is not what I want to do.* I respect doctors, but I knew early on it wasn't for me.

Ironically, for someone who hates needles, I ended up in a long-term relationship with an acupuncturist. That's right; she put needles into people for a living. In fact, I tried acupuncture myself and was a bit shocked to find that it worked. But I couldn't do that to somebody else. The other irony is that I also love tattoos, but I always look away during the process. So medicine was not for me, even if acupuncture and tattoos are.

Engineering

My dad, in his usual practice of parenting, gave me other ideas. He gave me books. We brainstormed together. As the oldest of his three sons, I would be the first to go out into the world, so he was pretty invested in my decision.

I read Ray Kurzweil and became fascinated by medical futurism. Kurzweil had accurately predicted a lot of technological advances that were already happening. I thought, *What would it mean to be human in twenty or thirty years, with AI, nanobots, and all these enhancements?*

And what would that mean for a guy like me picking a career? This wasn't sci-fi; it was real and exciting. The closest career path I could find was biomedical engineering, so I took that route.

Eventually, I learned that biomedical engineering wasn't right for me either. I did stem cell research at the University of Minnesota and worked at a pediatric medical device startup. I was in a lab every day, working on things that would take five to ten years to develop. I didn't feel like I was making a direct impact. Progress was slow, and the work was isolating. I never really talked to anyone outside the small team I was on.

That frustration led me to health care policy. I was still thinking about the predictions of medical futurism. I believed I could get meaningfully involved in discussing these important bioethical questions and issues. It would be fun, it would make a difference, and I would be interacting with people, not locked away in a lab.

So I got involved with the state of Minnesota, working on their health care policies. This was around the time of the Affordable Care Act. But I became disillusioned. I found that government entities were slow and unmotivated. People just wanted to get their benefits and then leave. It was draining for me.

I also didn't like that everything in health care was political. Whether it was Obamacare or the free market, the conversations seemed unproductive and had little impact. The debate disguised the real issues. I thought, and still think, that the core problem was consolidation. Big health care was replacing small providers. We were losing the local community doctor—the one with the black bag, who knew your name, and ate at the same restaurants as everyone else. I couldn't engineer anyone out of that situation, and I probably couldn't legislate a way out of it either. But I knew the solution had to involve the law.

Law

So I went to law school. I immersed myself in medical law. In many of my practice areas, there were few other attorneys doing what I was doing. Why, I don't know. But straight out of law school, although I hadn't connected all the dots, I knew I wanted to work for myself.

I started by negotiating medical bills and fighting health insurance appeals. It was a low-entry, lower-risk area, but I was fighting the bad guys, and that felt good. But it wasn't enough to make a real living. I had to subsidize my law practice by moonlighting or doing document review, which is the most boring legal project you can do.

From talking to other attorneys, I realized that small business law offered a much more predictable revenue stream. That's when it clicked: Small medical business owners are the people actually fighting big health care. They're entrepreneurs like me, and we need more entrepreneurs in the system.

Small, fresh, entrepreneurial, agile law firms would be more effective than big, old-school, slow-moving, institutional firms.

I got connected to the startup scene. But I didn't want to scrap my patient advocacy work, so I launched a startup called Cut Medical Bills with another David I met at a networking event. His mom was about to have surgery and needed a will. I helped him out, even though it wasn't my practice area.

He turned out to be really good at videos and websites, so we linked up. We were teaching people how to negotiate their medical bills and fight their health insurance appeals without an attorney. The business probably could have grown much bigger, but we never scaled it up. Back then, we were both kind of "do-it-yourselfers." We had no money, didn't ask for help, and knew little about e-commerce. We did our own little ads and networking. It was fun; we got some sales, but we didn't know enough for it to go where it could have. But I learned a lot, and the startup experience helped make me who I am today. David still runs that business on the side, while I pivoted into small business health care law.

It was fun to be in the startup scene. Being around other entrepreneurs and small business owners was illuminating. Just being around those people, you see the world differently. You ask better questions. You train your mind to see opportunities differently. You ask questions like, "Why do we do it that way?" "Why don't we do it this way?" I love that.

That experience still shapes the way I approach legal services. I'm not thinking about how other lawyers do things. Instead, I'm running a business that happens to be in law. The only limits when it comes to finding solutions are ethics, rules, and the law—not what all the lawyers before me did. For me, practice is about growth and innovation.

But Really, Who Am I?
I've practiced yoga. I've studied and practiced understanding the medical system. I've practiced law. I've practiced parenting. I'm always practicing—always trying to get better. That's who I am.

I'm a dad, a friend, and an entrepreneur in health care. When it's all said and done, I just happen to be a lawyer.

At the core, I'm addressing the reality that, in many ways, our health care system has room for improvement. My role is to make an impact on health care. I'm doing that through law and through my docu-health startup, by providing people with video training and other resources.

That's who I am: an entrepreneur making an impact on health care. Period.

The only question that's left to answer is this: Why should anyone trust me?

Here's why: I've been through the trenches. I've built out practice areas that no other lawyer has ever done. To do that, you need more than a good command of the law. You also need good risk intuition and solid business acumen. Those skills are vital to the kind of people I'm trying to help.

To be an entrepreneur in health care, you need to be a strategic thinker. That's what I've become. I will never be satisfied with the status quo. I love thinking three steps ahead for my clients. My job is to get out ahead of them, learn what they need to know, and help them gain perspective as they grow.

Chapter 2
The Second Law of Business Health: Gain Perspective

Practice is nonnegotiable if you want to succeed in business, whether that business is medical, legal, or something else entirely. But the *way* you practice is just as important. Think of this as the guidance or direction of your practice. Running hard is great, but knowing where you are heading is critical if you want to actually arrive at your destination. Again, you need practice to be excellent at something, but it has to be guided practice. And that guidance requires *perspective*. I've gained perspective from many life experiences, but none more so than travel.

Travel
When I was in middle school—sixth grade through the first half of ninth grade—I lived abroad with my family in Belgium. I was there during the 9/11 attacks. The experience showed me there's a lot more going on in the world than just the issues of the United States. I learned that there are many ways to think, eat, socialize, and enjoy life.

One thing I especially envied about European culture, particularly in the north, was how much time people spent with family. They worked less and ate long, sociable meals together. It felt like there were holidays every week.

Our school had half-days on Wednesdays, which was new to me. Such cultural differences, combined with being overseas during an event like 9/11, sharpened my understanding of my own country. Having an outside perspective of the United States changed the way I thought about our country. I stopped believing we were the best in the world and beyond criticism.

I met Europeans who offered valid critiques of the US. They were polite, but objective and direct. Listening to these perspectives helped me later in life to look at systems and say, "There are good things about this, but also things that are broken and need to change. And it's okay to talk about that."

I also learned French while we lived in Europe. I could speak at an intermediate level for a while. I wish I had kept at it longer. Learning a different language, like learning the law, was not easy. Consistency is the key. In language, as in law, you have to keep updating your knowledge and practicing. When you don't practice, your skills fade.

While practicing French, I learned that not all teachers are created equal. Some French teachers—and bilingual friends—taught me a lot. Others were less effective. A big part of my job now involves translating complicated legalese into English. Using formal legal language doesn't usually help the client absorb what they need to know. With legalese, as with French, it matters who your teacher is. Effective teachers know how to guide others.

Those soft skills, on top of advanced legal knowledge, are hard to gain except through experience. My experience is twofold. I have been shaped not only by being a lawyer, but also by being a business owner. From this unique position, I can speak directly to my clients' needs and help them stand out.

Travel also gave me a love of seeing new places and experiencing different cultures. I knew from a young age that I wanted to travel more. For me, the clearest route to that goal was becoming an entrepreneur. Owning my own business meant I could set my own schedule and move around freely. We traveled all over Europe while we lived there. My dad set a good example by prioritizing family travel. He didn't let finances or work get in the way. He focused on earning more so we could travel more, instead of complaining about the cost of travel.

Travel within the US has also given me new perspectives. My first trip to California was a weeklong family vacation that included a family gathering in Palm Springs. I loved being able to get away from winter weather. That trip became a tradition. And over the years, I realized I didn't have to stay where I was born. I could go anywhere, even if I had a child, a career, or family ties.

As a business owner, you have more opportunities to travel or live elsewhere. This was especially true during the COVID-19 pandemic, when so many people first learned to work remotely. Many years after that first California trip, I hitched a trailer to our car, sold our starter home, and drove there with my partner and our son. We bumped around in short-term rentals all over California, spending one month here and one month there. I worked remotely the whole time. In fact, it was one of my best, most productive business seasons.

I think COVID-19 challenged the status quo and people's assumptions about how to live life. It showed us the benefits of remote work. In a way, travel got easier. For me, being in a warmer climate during a depressing pandemic winter far outweighed the cost. Being able to say "Forget it; we can do this" was empowering. Even with a child, we could walk into the unknown. That builds the kind of confidence that says, "If I can do this, what else could I do?"

Just because you haven't done something before or someone else says it's too risky doesn't mean that's the case. Travel helped push me further into the entrepreneurial life.

Lending Perspective

Perspective is best when it's shared, in my experience. I've gained perspective from a lot of things in life, so now I can lend it to others, especially in law, medicine, and business. Some of my most fulfilling experiences have involved helping others with the perspectives I've gained, being the "French teacher," if you will.

I've been able to meet business owners where they are and then journey with them as we grow together. Those are the stories I look back on with real satisfaction.

A Community Healthcare Company

A Community Healthcare Company was founded by a community of immigrant entrepreneurs. A group of three entrepreneurs from the same tribe started with very little but were very action-oriented. They approached county representatives and worked hard to learn about the legal system related to health care and business.

They are persistent people—inspiring clients focused more on value than cost. They were able to build something from nothing. They started with only a business name and grew it into a seven-figure business in three years.

How did they do it? They started strategically with one health care service, then layered on more and more licenses over time. That's an ideal pathway for many of our new clients to follow.

We were able to be their gateway. They needed licenses so they could bill. We got them those licenses, and they started to generate revenue. Then they could grow, support their community in specific ways, and hire people from within their own community.

We gave them the benefit of our experience as they navigated a complex and ever-changing legal and regulatory system. They haven't looked back. Today, they are a fractional legal counsel client. They pay us monthly, and we take care of all of their legal needs. We also advise them in other areas.

With their hard work and our help, they have become the kind of success story most entrepreneurs dream about.

DIY Surgeon

The Doctor Client is an OB-GYN surgeon who has taken the entrepreneurial leap. He offers MEDSPA-type services for women in addition to traditional OB services. In our society, there's heavy pressure on women to look good, even more so than men. He helps women during and after pregnancy (which can be very taxing on the body) through his medical spa care.

He still attends deliveries and performs birth care, but now focuses on making sure women feel great about their bodies after birth. This could include skin treatments or vaginal procedures. His goal is to help women feel and look their best.

He's done very well, and he's very entrepreneurial. He told me, "I'm not just an OB-GYN. These women have a lot of issues before and after birth that I want to help solve. Because they're already here, I can do that as an MD and help them in many ways."

He came to us when his business was growing. Now he is a general counsel client. Although he's a smart guy who likes to get heavily involved with his contracts, we were able to help him get to that next level.

He already did an awesome job. But we layered on a few more steps we knew would add value for him. He's a surgeon, and I'm kind of a surgeon of lawyers. Experts like him shouldn't get caught up in work outside their expertise. It would be like if I started delivering babies. I might be able to doula for a while, but I should not be in charge of anyone's labor and delivery. There could be serious consequences if I messed up.

We've helped him start delegating more and entrusting more to his attorney instead of trying to DIY the law. His approach had taken him far in his practice, but we have been able to help him go farther. We encouraged him to focus on what only *he* can do.

I essentially said to him, "Go be the surgeon of health care. I'm going to be the surgeon of legal. We'll trust that you're good at your thing. You trust that I'm good at my thing, and we're going to save each other time." And it has worked.

Even when working with hands-on clients, we pride ourselves on streamlining communication and eliminating distractions and delays. When experts trust each other's expertise, everyone benefits. We each bring experience and perspective the other doesn't have.

We were able to help him optimize his business and focus on his goals. He didn't have to look at every single detail. When our clients trust our perspective, they can grow because they are free to focus on what they do best.

Pivotal Perspective

We helped another Doctor Client grow and pivot her business in ways she had only imagined. She came to us as she was leaving a prominent hospital position as a pediatric neurology specialist. Her work was intense and complex, caring for children with seizures and developmental disabilities. She had an encyclopedic knowledge of her field of medicine. But she had less knowledge of business and the law.

She told me, "I need to change."

She was mid-career and still in her prime. But she wanted to be able to do her own thing. We helped her start from scratch. We also helped her become an expert witness. She traveled the country doing that and made a lot of money, which helped subsidize her growing practice.

My job was to keep her out of any compliance trouble while she pursued her new path. She was the kind of doctor other doctors call when they have the most complex case. She got a reputation for taking on complex cases her colleagues would not, usually from fear of malpractice suits.

She didn't charge nearly as much as she should have. She was working with patients on medical assistance. These were incredibly complex, high-risk cases. And many parents, sadly, can be combative with their child's doctors, adding to the stress of these cases.

Even with all the complexities, we were able to help her set up a strong legal foundation. I still consider her a great friend.

Without our help, I suspect she would have stayed in the hospital or retired earlier. That would have meant many fewer pediatric neurology patients getting the care only she could provide. We provided another perspective that helped her see there was another way for her. There was a pivot to be made. We helped her see it was not only possible, but also better than her existing situation.

She could keep doing what she was great at. I got the legal figured out and provided some operational support so she could focus on her medical practice. Legal would not be a barrier to her starting a new chapter in her career. She felt empowered to keep going and to grow. That's what we love—helping people achieve their dreams.

Some clients, like the Community Healthcare Company, want to know what's possible when starting something from nothing. Other clients, like our Doctor Client, need some help letting go of the details. And some, like our other Doctor Client, are looking for a change but don't yet see how to make it happen.

These are just three examples of how we provide perspective for our clients. We bring not just legal know-how, but entrepreneurial know-how, connections, and vision. We help them craft their vision and implement it.

These are the kinds of stories we love being a part of. I help people and businesses grow, because growth is a central part of my philosophy.

Chapter 3
The Third Law of Business Health: Never Stop Growing

The third law of business health is simple: *Never stop growing.*

The question any healthy person or business should ask themselves is this: *Who am I becoming?*

Before you answer that question, I want to share how I've grown and invested, both personally and professionally. It all starts with our philosophy, which drives the ways we seek to grow. That helps us see what we want to change about our lives. I'm going to share my growth philosophy with you, and then it will be your turn to ask yourself: *How can I grow in my own personal and professional life? What does that look like for me?*

A Philosophy of Growth

I've become someone who never stops growing. That's true in my personal life, health care, law, and business. Even more, I've realized I have a calling of sorts to help others attain the same mindset. I believe this mindset can transform our entire health care system by empowering health care businesses to do the same: Never stop growing.

As I continue to seek growth in these areas, I see more and more clearly how connected they are. That's because they are all rooted in the same philosophy of growth. I want to share that philosophy with you and then help you apply it to your own personal and professional life.

Personal

I've already told you where my drive for personal growth started—my near-electrocution. That showed me one simple truth: Life is short.

Some people realize this truth through a death in the family—others through a worldwide event like a pandemic. Whenever or however you learn that truth, you can't ignore it.

It's an awful shame not to keep working on yourself. Being less than you can be does everyone around you a complete disservice, especially your kids.

Statistics clearly show that parents are the biggest predictor of their children's success. For me, my son Milo is a big motivator. If you are a parent or leader, you owe it to those who rely on you to become your best self. That might mean breaking some generational cycles.

This is not easy. It takes a raw, honest assessment of your life.

Even if I didn't have a child, and I was just talking about me, I think we all want to become better versions of ourselves. The question is this: *How do we light the fire and commit to real steps forward?*

I've learned that growth speeds up when we use *guides*. In every area of my life, I go to the best person who can help me. That person might be a personal trainer, marketing guy, business coach, yoga teacher, electrician, or even someone to help me write this book.

This has been an evolution in my philosophy. I've learned that I don't need to go and figure it all out by myself. Now I see the benefit of seeking help. Of course, some self-reflection is essential. But the right guides help you grow ten times faster. They will see the things you miss. They help you apply your philosophy in practical ways.

Aristotle taught this philosophy, called *virtue ethics*. It's about looking at the good life as a journey, not as a list of rules to follow or goals to achieve. It's about practicing virtues like courage, excellence, or generosity. Throughout the journey, through practice, you build this set of skills.

And if you practice this with others, in community—especially with mentors who are further down the road—you get better at it. It's like learning any instrument, sport, or skill. You get better through repetition and guidance.

The key is that you don't do any of this alone. You seek out people who have more expertise than you do. And you practice to become your best self. You owe that to your community, especially those closest to you. Especially the children and younger people who depend on you.

When you commit to growth and becoming your best self, everyone around you benefits. I believe this is the healthiest way to live.

Health

When it comes to our personal health—and the broader health system in our society—we owe it to ourselves to take responsibility. Health is a key part of a larger picture. And I'm not just talking about physical health. Physical health can get reduced to ego. It looks good, and you can see the results. But health also involves emotional growth. It means growing as a leader and changing how you react to your environment.

This often goes back to deeply ingrained patterns. Rewiring those synapses is hard, but it is possible. Change takes time. It takes hard work. And it takes a carefully thought-out plan. But it is possible.

More broadly, I take a hybrid approach to our US health care system. I see strengths in both major proposed solutions, but the argument often oversimplifies the issues at stake. One approach is the single-payer model, where the government pools all the money and solves the problem. The other major approach is a business-oriented, private market philosophy. Neither is perfect.

Whatever the system, I believe individuals are responsible for working on their own health. You don't have to do it alone. Use experts. Use a dietitian. Use a personal trainer, as I do. You can work out and eat better. You don't need to figure it out on your own, but you owe this to yourself, and it is your job to make the effort. Take the time. Go work out. No one *wants* to work out, but it's essential.

Often, I don't want to go to my own workouts, but I've made it a part of my routine. I know it makes me a better person. I'll have more energy for my son, and I'll feel better this weekend if I work out during the week. Still, it's easier to become distracted by our busy everyday lives than it is to take action.

I've seen this in my own organization. Time was the biggest excuse people had. So I created a program for my team to incentivize health. This dovetails with business growth, but it also supports personal and social well-being.

If you believe in your employees, you need to create a work environment that supports their health. Go beyond what the law requires. Don't stop at PTO. If you do the bare minimum, you're leaving growth on the table.

I'm doing this with my own firm, and I believe our growth over the next three, five, and ten years will prove that it works. We are going to be light-years ahead of our competitors because I'm investing heavily in the wellness of my people—and not just their physical health. I'm empowering them to take more responsibility as well.

We are adding a mindset trainer. This is not a therapist, but a coach. The mindset trainer is someone who supports the internal work people may have put off but always knew they needed. It's not about getting team members on board with company goals but to really help them see the world differently. It's about helping people grow.

I reject the philosophy that says, "You're on your own. Take care of your own benefits. You're pregnant? Figure it out." If we as business owners insist that free markets are the answer, we need to lead. We can't just say that government isn't the answer; we need to be the answer. Business owners need to step up and care for their people. That's health care leadership.

What are we actually doing to improve the health and well-being of our citizens? What are the health outcomes of our staff compared to the average person? These are questions business owners should be asking.

There are levels of responsibility. Personal responsibility—for your own health and your own actions—is just the start. We also bear responsibility to the people around us: our employees, our families, the people who depend on us. Finally, there is institutional responsibility, where government or large institutions do what can't be handled elsewhere.

Hopefully, individuals and smaller groups, like businesses and communities, will solve most of these problems. I think that's a compelling vision for the health care system.

We can grow—personally, professionally, and communally. I know it's possible because my company is already doing it.

Law

I've experienced growth through practicing the law and applying my philosophy to health care law in general. I refuse to stop finding ways to grow and innovate in this arena.

For example, we have been using artificial intelligence (AI) much more than most other law firms. We're integrating it into our services to make the client experience more pleasant. We can deliver services faster, and we're catching errors that a human might miss. Right out of the gate, we incorporated it into our current legal offerings.

My philosophy on AI is this: I look at it like any other business tool, like the internet or email. It's a set of tools that helps us grow. As we implement it, we will weigh the pros and cons, but I'm fully on board with continuing its integration into our services and growth strategy.

Honestly, I'd prefer that other attorneys allow themselves to be scared away from innovation, especially AI. That just gives me more opportunity to leave them behind, because of the increased value I can offer my clients.

If you want to grow as a business that deals with the law, you have to value innovation. But you also have to value the truth and practice radical honesty. One of my core values is living with integrity. And to be honest, I think it's the toughest one.

Doing the things you're supposed to do, even when no one's watching, is a practice. I get tempted all the time to just throw something in the trash instead of recycling. But I value not leaving this earth as a trash heap for my son when he's thirty-six. So I recycle, even when I don't feel like it. Even when no one can see.

When I think about integrity as a business owner, I ask, *What would I do if I weren't tied to the bare minimum that the law requires?* Nothing illegal, obviously, but what would I want to do? What would I implement in my workforce?

I talk with business owners all the time about the bare minimum. What's the least they have to do? What's the skin-and-bones version? I give them legal advice, of course, and I may not be their business advisor, but I always like to challenge that bare minimum mindset.

What if we provided more PTO than the law requires? Would we be able to attract and keep better workers? We have less turnover, so we have fewer issues. And even if we're only talking about money, you would make more money over the long term. But it takes a new approach and moving way beyond the bare minimum.

I want to think more creatively. I'm a business owner and entrepreneur. I have a team of staff. My PTO programs provide more real PTO than Apple, Tesla, or Google. We will grow in our legal practice by growing beyond what the law requires for our people. That will grow our business—and our clients' businesses.

Business

As a business, we are growing by finding creative ways to supercharge our people. We have done a PTO payback program. For some businesses, this may actually work better than unlimited

PTO, in which some team members may feel pressured to take fewer days off.

In a PTO payback system, if an employee doesn't use all those days, they get a fat cash payment at the end of the year. It's one of the most generous policies you can offer. The reason I do it is that I'm playing the long game—and the staff loves it.

I have the luxury to be able to do that because I'm further down the road as a business owner. Newer entrepreneurs may not have that luxury. Now, we are looking at improved models of unlimited PTO—models that don't discourage employees from taking days off. But PTO payback has worked well for us.

Here's how it works: An employee starts off with $8,000 in a kind of bank. A PTO day is worth $333.33. We let them take days off for nearly any reason. And what they don't use just banks at the end of the year.

Let's say I have one staff member who doesn't need much PTO. They're younger, single, and don't have kids. They're just looking to crush it at work. I don't force that on them, but I reward it. And the system doesn't penalize people who have kids and want to use more of their PTO. Everyone gets the benefits they need.

Unused funds don't have to be used for PTO. They can be used for other things, including wellness, tuition, and more. There's a tax advantage, so many people prefer to use the funds that way. Philosophically, I like putting the choice back in the employees' hands.

I like helping my staff to become *intrapreneurs*—entrepreneurs inside of the company. We all benefit from that. I want them to feel a part of the company. If they want to get their paralegal degree instead of taking more time off, they can use their PTO funds to do that. It's their call.

We are rethinking how we treat our people as a baseline. We take a thoughtful approach, applying my philosophy of personal, communal, and societal responsibility. We're building something that will last.

We're also innovating in tech—whether that's digital assistants or artificial intelligence. We're revising our policies, internal procedures, benefits, and systems to encourage growth. We want to be the most innovative team practicing law in health care. We want to be one of the most innovative businesses in America.

Holt Law is not afraid of innovation. We're not afraid to be the guinea pig. I'm putting my money where my mouth is, and I want you to see if I fail or succeed. And if you want to come along for the ride, you should do the same.

Integration for Growth

Obviously, my focus has been on health care law for years now. It's a niche. But is there a wider aperture here? Something that relates to entrepreneurship and, really, to all of life?

This process of innovation, this personal philosophy that drives our values, identifies things we think could be improved. We break them down to first principles. Then we use whatever tools, resources, or philosophical schemes are available in a given context to come up with a new way of addressing the opportunity.

We're innovating and iterating in health law, but also in the health care business. We're applying a kind of tech mindset that includes both personal and social responsibility. We're occupying a space where we can reach people anywhere. People who lean into personal responsibility. Bootstrap-type people. But also people who care about the planet, about society, about health outcomes.

We're working at a different level, away from the competing ideological visions of what health care should look like. It's an exciting place to be.

I was trained as an engineer, specifically in biomedical engineering. That's the mindset I bring to how I break down systems and test things. I break things to understand them. You rarely see engineers in law. When you do, they're usually in patent law. But an engineer who goes into law, then private practice, and then becomes an entrepreneur—that's an extremely rare pathway.

I used to wonder if that engineering degree was all a waste. But now it's all coming full circle. We're implementing the entrepreneurial operating system (EOS) model of business. We're breaking down broken legal systems and the health care system and saying, "Let's go backward and reengineer this from scratch."

We are integrating philosophy, personal, professional and business growth, and systems-level change. We want to innovate in every area. We use our philosophy of growth and the concept of iteration. That's how we approach problems, and we can apply our approach to a whole host of ideas and opportunities.

That's who we are becoming. How about you?

Who Are You Becoming?

When I'm guiding business owners—coaching, coming alongside them, trying to help them apply this way of thinking—I'm thinking about who they are becoming. Whether I'm working with health business owners or coaching through YouTube, I'm helping people apply this innovative personal, legal, and business philosophy to their lives. I want them to ask themselves, *"ho am I becoming?*

You owe it to yourself to become the best version of you. Most people, if they're honest, don't think they're quite there. And that's okay, because it's a process. It just takes execution and action. There are barriers. Nowadays, with screens and software everywhere, it's easy to land on a comfortable autopilot.

I've been there—personally, financially, and growth-wise. I was on a very comfortable autopilot.

I was cruising. But I wasn't growing. I was static. It was like *Groundhog Day*—rest, wake up, repeat, over and over. It got boring—until I was shocked out of it.

What I'm trying to do is accelerate an awakening that's probably already going to happen in your life. I do hope that it happens for you without you getting electrocuted or having to have that "I almost died" moment.

Getting to that reality—that clarity—starts by doing a raw, vulnerable self-assessment. It doesn't have to be some "journaling in the dark by yourself" journey. It can be a by-committee approach. I look at it as having a personal board of directors. I have guides: my business coach, marketing advisor, PT, sleep doctor, and more. I wrote it all down. Then I asked myself what I needed to do in each area to become my best self.

Step one is to take an honest personal inventory.

Step two is to write down the areas of your life you want to improve.

Step three is to build your personal board of directors.

Some people call it their "life team." Build your own suite of experts at whatever level you can. Their role is to help you grow faster in each area of your life. What comes after that? Iteration. Reflection.

With the help of these coaches or guides, you begin smart goal setting. To do that, you need to keep your motivation in the back of your mind. Mine was almost dying. And my son. I read my personal vision daily. That might seem like an advanced technique, but it's simple.

It's like writing a business vision, but personal. The key is to chart your path. It's not just manifesting and figuring out what you want to do. You need to put together a road map to get there. Then write it down. Sign it. Commit to it. When you sign your name on it, you're going to be less likely to let yourself down. It's a contract with yourself. And if you're not congruent in what you say and do, it creates a very uneasy feeling, at least for me. I suspect most people feel the same.

These are mechanisms of accountability: writing things down and having people in your life who are going to ask about your goals to hold you responsible. A personal trainer. A business coach. These people provide not just support but accountability and guidance. Another mechanism of accountability is announcing it to the world.

We posted a vivid vision for our company on our website. Our goals are big goals, but I want to hit them because it shows my team that my actions match my words.

It's the same with your personal goals. If they're written down, visible, and explicit, you won't want to let yourself down.

Facing Fears and Embracing Change

To grow, you also have to face your fears. Say you're terrified of AI, or you don't know anything about it. Ask yourself, Why? What does it represent for you?

AI has the power to transform the way we live. Every aspect of life, including health care, is in play. That can feel exciting or it can be scary, depending on the business owner. But the ability to accelerate your personal and professional growth is why you need to face AI head-on. This is a massive opportunity.

Some game-changing apps have been coming out recently. They look and feel like you have a coach built into the app, reading your emotions and looking at your behavior. This will touch on every area of life.

I have an AI vocal coach. It's fascinating the way it changes my plan, sends reminders, and catches me when I'm off. As I learn and grow, it changes the way it interacts with me. It's effective. I'm reaching my goals faster than I would have a few years ago. I also use it for personal and emotional development. Another AI app monitors my sleep patterns and activity. It makes some interesting suggestions, but what I like most is how it keeps my schedule organized. When I'm running around, being able to change things on the fly and get reminders is critical.

In my business, I use AI as a general organizational tool. I use it across the board. It's an elegant way to record stories—things I've always wanted to say—and turn them into text quickly, then produce a presentable form. I also use it to connect with more people. It's helping me become the best version of myself.

How could *you* imagine utilizing tools like AI in your life and business?

If you're a skilled practitioner in anything—lawyer, doctor, marketer, writer—you owe it to yourself to get in front of prospective clients. Bad marketing leads people to competitors who offer lower quality, where they may even pay more for worse service. So now I deeply respect good, clear, and concise marketing. I'm fully on board with marketing and sales. I now believe I have a duty to get in front of that doctor, med spa, or health care business, to prove that I am better than my competitors. AI helps our marketing serve us better so we can better serve our clients.

One of the most exciting aspects for our clients is how we integrate AI with our attorneys and law clerks. It double-checks and enhances our legal operations. It's like working with a third-year lawyer. It's not perfect, but bouncing ideas off it helps us. It also sparks creativity. Sometimes the AI's suggestion may be off, but it can lead to insight. This kind of collaboration strengthens our legal process.

I also use AI to expand my network on LinkedIn, connecting with people I wouldn't otherwise have time to find. It helps me communicate more efficiently. I use AI to craft emails and summarize long documents, like a sixty-eight-page lease, so I can focus on the key 20 percent that truly matters. This saves time and cuts through the boilerplate. AI cuts through layers of legalese and gets straight to the essence of a contract—something that frustrates most people.

Do you have processes in your business or personal life that you need to streamline?

For a small firm like ours, AI levels the playing field. We're a boutique firm with three attorneys, but we're growing quickly and plan to reach ten soon. AI allows us to compete with big law firms that used to be inaccessible unless you're part of the "right" network or can afford their steep costs. With AI, we can deliver better value—lower cost and higher quality. Big law firms, understandably, aren't thrilled. They are pushing back with ethical concerns and case precedents. But I see AI as a tool with more pros than cons. Of course, it must be used responsibly. Human professionals still need to fact-check cases and ensure accuracy. But business owners will have to embrace AI to stay competitive moving forward.

The beauty of AI is that it's easier to implement than a lot of people might think. Many popular applications already have built-in AI components. Google's Gemini summarizes emails and documents with little user effort. Zoom transcribes and summarizes meetings. Most CRM and software tools now have integrated AI features. AI technology has grown exponentially in just a few years and will continue to provide new and powerful tools for adding client value in the future.

So, for most businesses, it's not a question of *if* they'll use AI, but *when* and *how*. AI-enhanced services are becoming the default. Vendors will offer them as part of their service packages.

AI is more than just a new kind of tool set. It's a symbol of our philosophy—thoughtful risk-taking, innovation, testing, and optimization—for the good of our employees, our clients, and ultimately for the system itself. It's an example of how we will continue to face fear and embrace change. We will never stop growing. AI is one of the ways I embrace that philosophy in my life every day.

What about you?

How are you growing?

What new tools or resources are just waiting for you to embrace them?

What experts, coaches, or mentors can you reach out to as you take your next step toward the best version of yourself?

Chapter 4
The Fourth Law of Business Health: Don't DIY

I've already explained how I went from being a "do-it-yourself" guy—in my personal life and in my business—to someone who leans into coaching, training, and expertise. That includes both my own expertise and the expertise of others who can accelerate my growth and save me time, money, and energy.

When it comes to understanding the law—especially health law—you do not want to go it alone. Not everyone is ready to hire a legal expert today. Maybe you are still wondering whether you even need a health care business lawyer.

If you want to learn more about the law as it relates to health care businesses, you've come to the right place. Even if we never work together, I want you to walk away from this chapter with valuable knowledge about this dynamic area of the law.

The Nuts and Bolts of Health Care Law

I practice law in Minnesota and California, but I also help people understand and navigate federal law. That's because of the way our health care system is structured.

There is much more to health care law than any reader of this book would want to know. But for your purposes, I want you to think about health care business law in terms of two major categories: challenges and opportunities.

Challenges

The challenges that owners of health care businesses encounter are endless. But the legal challenges usually involve entity choice, traps (like referrals), file administration (including confidentiality), growth (employment and training), and ownership disputes.

Let's address these challenges one at a time.

Entity Choice

The first legal challenge health care business owners face is *entity choice*. It's inescapable if you want to do this kind of business in the United States: You need a legal entity.

Why? Because a legal entity serves as a shield for your liability. In a limited liability company, you're limiting your personal liability. This means that if something goes wrong, such as someone being harmed in a medical setting, you need protection.

Let's say something bad happens, and your malpractice insurance doesn't cover the situation. Now your business owes money to someone. If your limited liability company (LLC) or entity is set up properly, your liability will be limited to the business and what the business owes. You will not be personally responsible for the debt.

In other words, unless you've signed a personal guarantee or another exception applies, you are personally protected. This is a big deal. If your business make a big mistake, with significant financial exposure, it's going to stay within the entity. The entity might shut down, but your personal assets will be protected. Your money, your car, your house—everything you own—can't be touched.

Personally, I think this is a gift to business owners. It's not a license to take risks, but a protective backstop against something unforeseen happening.

Entity choice gets interesting for a health care provider. In Minnesota and California, for example, we have respective rules and acts for professional firms. That means medical professionals have the option, and potentially the requirement, to create a professional entity. Lawyers and medical professionals in these states can use a "P" in front of their entity name and identify themselves as a professional corporation instead of a standard one. In some cases, this is optional; in others, it's required.

The key here is that medical companies in general must be owned by licensed professionals. We can't have a layperson—say, a savvy business investor—owning 99 percent of a medical clinic with a doctor owning the remaining 1 percent. At least, not in California and Minnesota. There *are* legal loopholes, which I'll cover later.

Each situation is different. But from experience, the majority of the entities I file are LLCs. The exception is California, which does not allow professionals to use LLCs. I'm not sure why—California is an interesting state.

Statistically, LLCs comprise the majority of entities filed in Minnesota. There's a reason for that. Many of these are filed with sound legal advice; some are not. I'm not providing legal advice in this book. But if you're following what most well-advised professionals are doing, they're probably filing LLCs.

One advantage is that an LLC gives you flexibility in how you are taxed. People often ask about filing as an S corp, but an S corp is not a legal entity. An S corp is a tax election, not an entity in itself.

For example, Holt Law is an LLC in Minnesota, but I've made the S corp election for tax purposes. I'm taxed as an S corp, but my legal entity is still an LLC.

All of this means that an LLC will likely be your entity of choice. As a medical professional, you may also need to make a professional election. In Minnesota, a doctor's professional designation would be medicine and surgery. For a nurse, the designation would be nursing, or in Minnesota, registered nursing, which can be confusing because it also applies to the other nursing designations.

There are certainly other choices beyond the LLC, such as limited liability partnerships, but we're not going to spend much time there. I want to point you toward the most likely best fit without giving you a legal treatise on every entity choice available.

Absent unique concerns or unique goals—like creating an investable startup, founding a nonprofit, or establishing a hospital system—an LLC will most likely be your entity of choice.

And once you have chosen your entity, you need to know about traps.

Traps

In health care, unlike many other businesses, there are a lot of specific rules. At both federal and state levels, there are regulations about how you pay for referrals, how you split fees (whether with your staff or with other professionals), how you advertise, how you protect information . . . the list goes on and on.

In a less-regulated business, such as e-commerce, you can incentivize other people, provide referrals with limited exceptions, and do affiliate marketing, where if someone sells your product, they get a cut. That's a form of fee splitting, which is allowed in many industries but not in health care.

Why not? If you look at the federal regulations—and those in states like Minnesota and California, the reason becomes clear. Too much referral, fee splitting, or incentivized driving of traffic can interfere with how patients choose their providers. There are too many business hands in the pot. So there are strict rules on receiving referrals. In general, assume they should not be incentivized.

But that doesn't mean that I can't have strong referral relationships. If I'm a medical doctor with a strong relationship with a prescriber who provides therapy, I can refer patients to them. We just have to follow the rules.

Fee splitting is another example. Suppose I provide a service, receive payment, and then split the fee with the person who sent me the client. This is often called a kickback. They send me a patient, I make money, and I kick back some of the money to thank them. This is not allowed when we're dealing with physician-based services or anything publicly funded—Medicare, Medicaid, or Tricare. There may be nuances when we're dealing with nonphysician services, but generally speaking, no public dollars, no kickbacks.

You'll see this in the cosmetic aesthetic and medical spa world. There, you might get away with what might be considered traditional fee splitting, but it has to be done in a very specific way. Best practice here is to have an attorney walk you through the federal and state regulations and your actual arrangement. Even the dollar amount has been cited by federal regulatory authorities.

Attorneys have helped carve out exceptions to these rules. We call these "safe harbors." These safe harbors allow you to do—under very specific conditions—what would otherwise be a kickback or fee split. These carve-outs usually have dozens of specific provisions. That's why legal advice is essential.

As long as we stay within the lines, the government has decided these activities are okay. The businesses that learn to navigate these traps have the best growth potential. They develop a competitive advantage over their counterparts who just throw their hands up and avoid the issue.

Some providers choose to live in fear or operate in a very cautious manner. That's fine. But with a little calculated risk and a clear interpretation of the rules, you can win big.

With the help of an attorney, you could be setting up an incentivized system: a discount program, a legal referral system, or maybe even what looks like a fee split but is done with safe harbor rules. This is how you leap ahead of your competition.

So yes, there are traps. But knowing how to navigate those traps can give you an advantage over your counterparts. And one of the biggest traps is *file administration*, which is all about confidentiality and relates directly to concerns about health care marketing.

File Administration (Confidentiality)
Online reviews are huge.

In 2024, the FTC came out with updated rules about reviews—what we can and can't do, best practices, and what they will enforce from now on. This was a major update. They addressed modern e-commerce and acknowledged the way it overlaps with health care.

There is a lot of telehealth. There are many blended businesses. There are Google and Facebook reviews. People are producing videos using patient testimonials, which I think is huge. But all of this needs to be done correctly. That's the trap for health care professionals.

In most other industries, you have more leeway, as long as you're not deceptive or fraudulent. But health care is different, and there are more rules for health care professionals.

In health care, there is an added layer of regulations about overstating your qualifications or the power of your services. What usually gets providers in trouble is implying that they can cure certain ailments through their services.

As in law, there is a rule that one patient's result does not guarantee the same result for other patients. Claims about results must be backed up by documented, transparent data. You'll see this often with medical devices. Advertising messages may share a positive patient experience, but the ad always ends with "results may vary."

Health care marketing receives high scrutiny. And this relates to another trap: maintaining confidentiality and protecting patient health information.

Patient records and information must remain confidential. But if I provide you with a testimonial, whether it's video, written, or in another form, I'm clearly acknowledging that I'm a patient. That means we need clear, strict rules of engagement. You need written documentation that a patient gave consent to share their story and a process for withdrawing that consent if the patient doesn't like how their testimony is used.

These are strict rules of engagement, but also smart legal practices. Not every lawyer gives you both the legal requirements *and* strategic advice about your options. We offer our clients a focus on long-term business strategy. This usually means helping them grow while taking calculated risks.

Many health care businesses believe they can't get Google reviews. They assume they can never use patient testimonials and that everything needs to stay locked in a vault. So they feel they can't let the world know how many people they've treated or how great a job they've done.

I say it's the opposite.

You *should* be sharing stories of the people you've helped. It's true there are extra rules. And when health care providers try to DIY this instead of consulting experts, they can get into trouble. They get burned and back away, leaving behind a missed opportunity.

What makes this such a missed opportunity is that search engines reward those with public reviews. When gathered properly and correctly, reviews can put you far ahead of your competition.

Again, this is a trap that can turn into a reward, once you understand the limits of the trap and find the leeway that allows you to take action. Very few professionals in the industry do this. They say it's too complicated. They don't want to figure it out, so they make the safe choice, which is to do nothing. But doing nothing leaves opportunity on the table.

In general, federal HIPAA rules safeguard patients' health care information. Additionally, some states—like Minnesota and California—add additional layers of regulation. When state law is more stringent than federal law, it takes precedence.

So in general, we need to keep health care information confidential. The first gateway that can give you a big advantage is knowing what constitutes *protected* health information.

We are required to keep all *protected* health information confidential. What does this mean?

For example, names and phone numbers are *not* protected health information. So if you consent to text reminders, we can email you about additional services that our med spa is going to provide. Other industries do this all the time; your inbox is probably full of examples.

Health care has a strict higher threshold. Your email marketing list requires a formal opt-in, and the opt-out must be done carefully as well.

Because we're dealing with protected health information, smart health care and business attorneys lay all of this out in their *Notice of Privacy Practices*. This is the document no one ever reads when they go to a health care provider. It's full of HIPAA terms and legalese.

Most providers don't read it either. But I have. I usually draft them.

Here's a key: Very few attorneys have updated these documents to reflect the way we actually practice medicine today. That includes telehealth, email and text communications, new software, and the marketing of new services that patients actually *want* to know about.

But businesses tiptoe around it. They're not sure if they can actually send such information, because they are worried about HIPAA regulations and protected health information.

Everyone thinks they know what HIPAA means. They can recite versions of the rule. But very few health care attorneys know the rule from start to finish.

Now, I admit there are nuances to the rules that rarely come up. They are seldom even dealt with in the law. But there are opportunities.

Once again, here's the theme: If you understand exactly what HIPAA and the state privacy laws say, you can purposely build consent into your forms. For example, you can give patients the option to receive texts or emails. Normally, these would not be allowed because they are not secure and not technically HIPAA-compliant. But patients do want them.

I love getting those text reminders. With my busy schedule, they're a big help.

But what about marketing new services?

People may say, "I love this medical spa. I see they're doing Botox. I would love to know if they start doing microneedling or laser treatments." They might even say, "I really love the owner and would like to get emails from them."

You can do that; you just have to follow the rules.

Here's the trap: When you send marketing emails, you must always use blind carbon copying (BCC). You can't allow a patient to see other patients' names and email addresses. That is generally one of the most common HIPAA breaches.

When it comes to confidentiality, we need both physical and technical safeguards to protect patient health information.

Nowadays, we're dealing with software, and most of it is encrypted. You put in your password and you're good to go. Modern software is powerful—especially in bigger companies that monitor every log-in and track every keystroke. You can't sneak into and out of a digital room without being noticed. Access is restricted.

Smaller businesses can still run into issues. Maybe you are using independent contractors, or you have employees who haven't had proper HIPAA training. Or perhaps you are working with a third-party vendor, like a billing company, that needs access to protected patient information to do their job.

If that's the case, you must have a *business associate agreement* in place. This is a legal agreement that sets out the rules for your vendor: This company agrees to follow HIPAA, understands the rules, and accepts shared liability. If something goes wrong or if there is an audit, this is what you both are going to do, and the other company is also responsible.

This agreement provides a legal highway for protected health information to flow between your medical company and another party.

These systems and legal structures matter. Doing it right, with expert counsel, is how you protect your business. It's how you focus on what you do best.

And it's how you grow your business.

Growth

For our health care business, as for most businesses, growth is on everyone's mind. Growth can take different forms, but when I think about it, I'm specifically thinking of staff.

Health care professionals are limited in their time. Many can fall into the common startup trap of trading time for revenue. This often leads to burnout and potentially business failure, because the owner can't focus on what they're really good at. Surgeons, for example, are the only ones who can do the surgeries that make their practice possible. They shouldn't be the one taking a patient's blood pressure.

In many cases, a surgeon comes into the operating room, performs the surgery, and leaves. Often, the surgery is quicker than expected. If you look at some of the best surgeons in the world and how many procedures they do in a day, it's amazing. When they arrive, the patient is already prepped. The nurses are ready, the machines are ready, and everything is set.

The surgeon doesn't go to the waiting room to greet you. They don't grab coffee with you. They don't take your blood pressure, set up the operating room, sanitize all the instruments, or get all the numbers in order. They walk in, pick up their scalpel, perform the surgery, get out, and get briefed for the next case.

I think this analogy is helpful. In a perfect world, as a health care professional, you would only be doing the surgery—or the procedure or service—that only you can do. But in a startup, it's usually just you doing everything.

So the question is this: How can we—quickly but safely, in compliance but without too much risk—get you from filling all the roles to doing "only surgery"? The best approach for most owners is a layered one. It depends on your tolerance for risk when it comes to hiring or engaging staff.

In general, there are three main ways to add staff.

The first is using a staffing agency. A staffing agency takes on all the HR risk and places people in your company. You pay the agency, they handle all the nuances of employment law, and you get prescreened people quickly.

You can also use virtual assistants, usually based abroad. Compared to the US minimum wage, they are very economical and growth-friendly. This can take much of the administrative burden off your plate. The downside of this approach is cost. You pay an elevated rate because the staffing agency needs to get paid too. So you are paying more than what the worker actually receives.

This is the price of doing business; it is what it is.

If you're working with a staffing agency to place a clinician, expect the cost to be even higher. Health care staffing is highly variable. Agencies take that issue off your plate, but there is a cost. The number one complaint I hear about staffing agencies is that they charge too much. In reality, they are charging what the market will bear, which is quite a bit.

The second option is employment. Small businesses do not need to fear adding employees.

It's easier than most people think. There are state-specific nuances, but I can teach you general concepts and key points of federal employment law.

Employees are under your direction and control. Whether employees are part-time or full-time, the employer provides training, directs the work, handles discipline, and provides the tools to do the job. Employees have legal protections: sick leave, PTO, breaks, anti-discrimination laws, overtime, and minimum wage. A small business owner can find all this intimidating.

There are also rules about getting the system all set up: state and federal taxes, payroll systems, and tracking requirements. Your CPA will tell you all the things you need to check. At first it may seem more expensive than hiring a contractor. That's why many small businesses shy away from bringing on new employees.

But if you're looking to grow quickly, you probably need to hire employees.

Personally, one of my biggest regrets as a business owner is that I didn't hire employees sooner. I relied on contractors and my own labor for too long. Only later did I start hiring employees and using virtual assistants.

Adding staff not only drives growth, but it also gives you back your time. It helps protect your mental health. It helps you stop working sixty to eighty hours a week just to keep the business afloat. Adding employees is not as complicated as people make it out to be. If you're serious about your business long term, it's worth the risk.

Finally, there are independent contractors. I like to think of them as hired guns—or pirates.

Say you're in a war. France is at war with England again. Instead of sending in our own military, we decide to take a chest of gold and pay a pirate army to sail in from wherever they are and assist us in our war.

The pirates bring their own ship. They bring their own people; they have their own sails, so they're ready to go. It's a simple exchange of money for services.

That's the key difference between contractors and employees. With an employee, you provide the training, tools, and infrastructure. You're supplying the ship and the means to operate it. Contractors come pretrained; they already know how to wage war. They're ready to go; they just need money.

What gets small business owners into trouble is failing to understand that difference. It can get further complicated because state and federal rules sometimes conflict with each other. There is usually a multifactor test that creates a gray area in determining who qualifies as a contractor.

This is where you need a good business attorney. You want someone who can say confidently, "This is an employee," or "This is a contractor," or maybe even, "We're operating purposely in a gray area, and this is why." Your attorney can outline your entire argument in case a regulator shows up at your door.

This is your first line of defense. Having an expert—your attorney—put their name, reputation, and malpractice insurance behind that opinion has real value. If a staff member's designation is incorrect, at least you have someone accountable.

To return to the pirate analogy: The pirates have their own ship. Contractors should provide their own tools—their own computer or laptop, internet access, and any other materials they need to do their job. I would even say that an independent contractor should also have their own entity. Then your company hires their company, and it's a business-to-business relationship.

This establishes them as a "hired gun." If you engage someone as an individual contractor, it might look and feel like they are an employee. If possible, you want the distinction of a contractor having their own entity. This can prevent messy situations down the road.

And speaking of messes, there are few situations messier than ownership disputes.

Ownership Disputes

Ownership disputes in health care are common. Just as in personal relationships, when you have more than one owner of a company, there is the possibility of a business divorce. These are common—and costly. Everyone's fighting for money, and the conflict can disrupt the business or even shut it down completely.

One way to mitigate this risk is to create something like a "prenuptial agreement" for any business partnership you are entering.

This document determines what happens if there's a fight or if someone wants to leave. It can cover dozens of events, like disability, divorce, retirement, and such. We have buy and sell provisions to answer questions like, if one of us leaves, how would that work? Can they get bought out? Is that even allowed?

All of this can be addressed in a "business prenup" or ownership agreement. If a dispute arises, there's no need to guess or argue. You just follow the agreement you made when you started the business.

This saves time and money. For new business owners who haven't been through an actual sale or a business breakup, it provides essential clarity. Think of it as a legal road map of what to do if the partnership changes.

Many clients approach me with no legal road map at all. They did the initial filing, but there's no actual written agreement between them and the other owners. Then a dispute happens. Maybe one of them is claiming to be an owner, but they may not be.

Now, the default is bad common law and unpredictable litigation. You go to court with a classic "he said, she said" scenario. You need every shred of written evidence you can scrape together to build your case. It's incredibly stressful and expensive. It's also preventable.

Avoid this at all costs.

A well-versed business and health care attorney is good at preventing ownership disputes before they happen. In many cases, the attorney can even serve to mediate or arbitrate the dispute informally.

Here's an example. In a small business, some owners are probably working more than others. That's common, and that's okay. When you're a small business, you're not only the owner. You're also probably doing the administrative work, along with providing actual professional services. But what you can do—with the right structure—is be both an owner and an employee of your own company.

Let's say you have two owners. One is strictly a financier—they put in money, want to get their investment back, and receive annual dividends if the business does well. The other owner also puts in money, but in addition, they work actively in the business—answering phones, administering the Botox, and generally doing the things that keep the business running.

Through an employment agreement, we can pay the working owner a fair market value for their work. Then, at the end of the year, after all the business expenses and salaries have been paid, we can split the profit if it's a 50-50 ownership. That way, the person doing more of the work is paid fairly; they get their employment salary and distribution.

Having those tough conversations on the front end, before you're at the breakup point, is where a highly skilled attorney can be invaluable. Among health care professionals, ownership disputes are made even more complex by additional obligations. It's not that easy to change ownership whenever and however you may want. If Medicaid or Medicare funds are involved, there are federal requirements around ownership reporting.

In many health care businesses, every time you change your ownership, you have to notify the government. You have to submit filings—a byzantine process of forms and regulations. If you do it incorrectly, it could disrupt your billing. That puts your payments from insurers or the government at risk. Your ownership dispute is not only painful and expensive, but it could also bankrupt the business (or what's left of it).

You want to do everything in your power to avoid that.

Ownership disputes in health care carry a lot of nuance, especially in health care law. One of the most valuable things you're paying for in a good health care business is the ownership setup, more so than the documents themselves. It's understanding what they mean, how they protect you, and when they might come into play.

This educational component is vital. Good attorneys do more than draft the agreement—they also explain it in plain English. When people understand the more complicated provisions, they see how this can save them significant amounts of money later. It's worth the investment.

It's like taking care of your health. If you're eating right and working out in your younger years, that's going to pay dividends later in life. If you wait until your later years to finally focus on your health or fitness, your options are more limited. Business works the same way.

It's not just about dealing with potential challenges. There are also opportunities to be had—if you know the law.

Opportunities

A more uplifting area of legal practice for health business lawyers is the land of opportunities—getting ahead of future changes, buying, and selling. These are proactive measures we can take to help you grow your business and enjoy the fruits of your labor.

Getting Ahead of Future Changes

In the post-pandemic world, we now live in a robust remote telehealth ecosystem. Some practitioners—generally medical spas performing physical procedures—have to carry out services in person. But many others, even the med spa providers, can do pre-visits and follow-up visits via telehealth. So it's essential to have a strong legal understanding of telehealth.

This area is evolving rapidly. During the pandemic, we saw a big push to make telehealth easy. We could cross state lines, bill for services, and get paid right away. But since then, we've slowly seen the old rules come back into play. At both the state and federal levels, there's ongoing debate about the future of telehealth.

Practitioners who understand properly what they can do and what they can't do across state lines will have a significant advantage. For example, suppose your patient lives in Minnesota, but drives to their cabin in Wisconsin—and you, the provider, happen to be on a plane or in the Bahamas. Three different sets of rules could apply: Wisconsin's telehealth rules, Minnesota's telehealth rules, and potentially federal or international telehealth and HIPAA laws.

Having a health care attorney who understands telehealth, telemedicine, and HIPAA—and looks proactively at opportunities to reach more patients—is crucial. It has become easy to open another practice location using the internet, remote offices, or virtual addresses that meet legal requirements. This allows providers to practice in multiple states without being physically present.

Understanding the minimum requirements and the consequences of setting up a new location is a huge advantage. But you have to know the legal nuances. For example, we've already covered marketing. Knowing the exact rules and gray areas of marketing and being able to navigate those confidently gives providers a competitive advantage. It helps them generate more revenue and achieve more success.

Additionally, with the internet and digital tools like courses, products, and social media, health care professionals have an opportunity not just to practice medicine, but also to reach more people through training or consulting.

This could look like a nurse consulting or training other nurses on how to do a procedure. Or it might be a nurse teaching other nurses how to grow a practice or showing other nurses or doctors how to address a specific patient situation. They can be a kind of ghost doctor. These business models are becoming more and more viable.

Expert witnesses are also creating digital products like books, videos, and affiliate marketing offerings. Many of these services involve fee splitting with other related disciplines.

For example, maybe you're a nurse and you have a colleague who's an MD. You frequently refer clients back and forth and eventually create a co-brand that generates revenue for both of you. You profit from a joint relationship without owning the same business. These are opportunities for alternative income streams.

But a lot of this hinges on knowing exactly where the practice of medicine starts and stops—and where the gray areas are. You'll see health coaches and even unlicensed individuals in this space, along with health care practitioners. There are real opportunities here but also real legal risk. You need sound legal advice you can rely upon.

Consider this example: A medical doctor wants to treat fewer individual patients and start a patient support group. They might bill for group services, offer educational videos, and share their skilled knowledge with more people. But they're not practicing medicine individually with each of these people. So what are the legal implications?

How do we do this right?

I love health care professionals who are thinking this way. I've done something similar in law, packaging parts of what I do into educational products that sell while I sleep. This is passive income that you create once. You do it well, and then people can buy it a million times online. Technological innovation has made it much easier to create digital courses and videos.

There's no reason for health care professionals to miss these opportunities. But you have to get the legal aspects right. The unlicensed practice of medicine, therapy, or mindset coaching can be anything from a misdemeanor all the way up to a felony in some states. That's criminal, not civil, in addition to civil penalties for any damages.

If you are unlicensed and telling people with cancer or another serious condition that a certain massage or lifestyle can make them healthier, you're getting dangerously close to the line. That might cross into saying you can treat a condition or do something that has been reserved for licensed professionals.

It's important to get this right if you want to participate in the future of health care business.

Purchasing Practices

A health care business is like any business; it can be bought or sold. But the complexity of the transaction all depends on the types of licenses. This isn't like selling a lemonade stand, a car dealership, or even an Etsy store. In health care, any change of ownership often requires multiple layers of reporting levels. Medicaid, Medicare, government entities, medical boards, insurance companies, and the local Secretary of State may all be involved.

So if this is done wrong, the consequences can be disastrous.

For example, suppose I start a medical practice staffed by MDs. If I sell my business to nurses—or to a combination of laypeople, chiropractors, and therapists—I could be in violation of multiple regulations. Why? Because under the corporate practice of medicine doctrine, only certain licensed professionals can legally own a medical practice.

So you need the appropriate licensed professionals to make the sale work. The corporate practice of medicine doctrine and the professional firms rule prevent unlicensed persons from owning medical practices.

There is a workaround, the *management services agreement*, that can allow unlicensed individuals to participate in a purchase or sale of a health care practice, but you need an expert who thoroughly understands the legalities.

This legal structure, a management certificate services agreement or management services organization, is a legal way to put one company in control of another—the medical practice—without transferring ownership. If done correctly, this company can then profit from the practice.

It takes a skilled health care and business attorney to structure this properly, because you're essentially trying to mimic ownership without actual ownership. The government does not love that, so you have to be extremely careful.

But if we follow the rules, we're good to go. When you are purchasing a health care business, a health care attorney adds value just as your realtor does when you are buying a house.

When you are looking to buy a house, everything looks good at first. You're driving by the house, studying the exterior, and reviewing the listing. The sellers took really nice pictures. They may have overstated a few things. Their realtor is marketing it to get the highest possible price.

It's the same when you're buying a business. The information you get from talking with a colleague, friend, or broker—or even browsing online—will be limited. What the attorney does is ask the tough questions. They will request tax returns, contracts, and other documents. Call it due diligence.

Consider this legal due diligence to be the equivalent of a home inspection. If you've ever bought a home, you know how important the home inspection is. It's a big deal.

Legal due diligence is like having somebody go through the property, inspecting every coat of paint and every plank of wood, then identifying every single plant in the yard. This is how you know exactly what we're buying.

Honestly, attorneys don't love doing due diligence. But it is *always* worth it.

The beauty of it is this: The attorneys almost always pay for themselves. We can often bring down the purchase price by identifying weaknesses or issues that are undisclosed or underdisclosed—intentionally or not—by the seller.

Sometimes a seller shows good faith. They'll say, "I'm going to tell you everything I know, good and bad. I'm putting it all on the table." I like those situations, but they are rare.

Today I see a new way of practicing law, one I hope continues to grow. The end goal is for the seller to sell to the buyer at a reasonable rate. Because we want a smooth transition, without burning any bridges, we try to disclose as much as we can up front. It's not like dealing with a massive Fortune 500 company where you battle it out.

I think these collaborative approaches are the most effective. I hope that this approach to practicing law continues to grow throughout the 2020s and 2030s.

For the buyer, once we've done our due diligence, the key is safely and effectively transferring the "keys to the castle" from the seller to the buyer. But while that's happening, the business is still functioning. Money is being preapproved. The business attorney keeps all of that moving forward.

And if something goes off the rails, we determine how serious the problem is and whether we can fix it. A good attorney does all of that and more. They also help manage expectations.

Some days, I'm just an extremely well-paid therapist. Buying or selling a business is often part of a major life transition, with all attendant emotional turmoil. People may be going through a divorce. Maybe they are letting go of a business to do something different in their life. Maybe there's a new baby in the family. Whatever the circumstances of the transaction, the consequences are not only financial but also emotional.

So, there's usually a lot going on during a purchase. A lot of feelings and concerns can get dumped into those conversations. That's why attorneys are sometimes called *counselors*. We don't just interpret the law. We also deal with everything that relates to the transaction, including the motives and emotions.

And then, of course, there's the paperwork.

On the buyer's side, many documents come into play. The main one is the *asset purchase agreement*.

You don't have to buy the ownership of a business outright. You can just buy all the pieces—the assets. That's an asset purchase.

Suppose I walk into a furnished home. I don't love the neighborhood, but the furniture is beautiful. So I say, "I would like to offer you this much for the furniture. I'll have my mover come out and pick it all up." That would be an asset purchase. I'm not buying the house; I'm just buying what's inside.

You can do the same thing with a business. And you can take the valuable pieces out of a business in this way.

An asset purchase can be a smart strategy. But as always in health care, you have to proceed carefully because many desirable assets are tied to professional licenses. Some licenses can't be sold as a stand-alone asset. They may be tied to the property or the original company. So you need to understand all the legal implications—or work with someone who does.

There are also these pesky things called National Provider Identification (NPI) numbers and a federal Employer Identification Number (EIN) that you have to consider. Do these come with the transaction? Can they even be sold? You need someone who understands all that and can say "Yes," "No," or "Here's what we need to do."

There are layers and layers of what you *can* and *can't* buy in a health care business. This is where the difference between a general business attorney and a health care business attorney is significant.

A general business attorney should know to check for licenses or business assets. But a business attorney with health care experience will already know the dozens of specific factors to consider. They'll be able to quickly identify which three actually apply to your transaction and advise on how serious it is if the previous owner erred on one of their filings that you now have to fix.

This kind of knowledge and skill saves time. It avoids surprises and keeps the deal on track. You're paying for that skilled labor, and it's worth it.

On a tight timeline, even a skilled attorney may not have enough time to research the complexities of a health care transaction or reach out to a colleague for answers. So personally, I avoid random buy/sell business transactions because they can take a lot of different turns.

Instead, I have created limited scope flat-fee packages. If you want to work with us, you're going to play by our attorney rules. We won't just jump into some haphazard situation on an hourly rate. We'll work for a flat fee and outline up front exactly what we're going to do.

Because of this, I turn away quite a few purchase and sales transactions. Often, people are trying to move too fast. They're not doing it the way that it should be done, and I know it won't end well. I don't want to be the one who has to deliver bad news—or put stress on myself and my staff because someone else is making poor decisions. That leads to conflict during and after the deal.

These transactions are risky for everyone. Especially for the buyer, who is often left to clean up the mess afterward.

In a business purchase, you're also taking on the staff and all the contracts. That means you're inheriting people. Some of them won't know if they're staying or if you're going to change everything. So dealing with the staff is particularly important.

A good business attorney does more than draft contracts to protect your interests. They also craft legally sound communications for staff and anyone else who needs to be notified. It's like legal PR.

Skilled business attorneys know how to work with everyone involved—all of the ancillary players who come into these transactions. That includes your team, your marketing folks, the new business owners—even spouses, who often jump on the calls. You have to know everyone who's in the deal. Who's paying? Who's a silent owner without being named?

Navigating all of these pieces—along with the conflicts and nuances that come with them—is a skill. That skill comes from doing this over and over again.

Health care business purchases often involve a jumble of contracts: licenses, employment contracts, ownership agreements, internal policies and procedures. If you have the policies well documented, you already have all the instructions for keeping the business afloat. If you don't have that documentation—or you lose a key employee who was handling all that—you might lose essential knowledge. That can cost real money and reduce the value of the business.

When it comes to buying a business, expertise matters. It also matters when you're selling one.

Selling

I think what's unique about how I practice as an attorney is that I've implemented standard operating protocols and understand the EOS model, a six-component method used to help businesses create solid foundations and improve current operations.

If I were looking to buy a business, I would want to make sure that when the previous owners are stripped out, we keep everything else intact. All the marketing, all the delivery of services, creation of the widgets, or whatever the business does—should be automated. There should be clear instructions so people can come in, read the instructions, and do everything that needs to be done.

I want to build systems so the business isn't reliant on David Holt—or anyone else—to come in every day. It could be anyone with a license.

Having that mindset when approaching a purchase or sale means I get to add unique value. I provide business advice in addition to legal advice; our clients have found that helpful. It also throws off other attorneys—or buyers and sellers—when I start speaking like an entrepreneur. Not all attorneys are business owners, and very few are entrepreneurs. In fact, most have never started a business.

I would argue, and I'm sure this will upset a few of my colleagues, that a good business attorney should have started a business. Period.

In my view, it's hard to provide truly strategic legal advice if you haven't built a business yourself. I've started and grown multiple companies, and that experience shapes how I guide clients.

When you've been in the same position—launching something from the ground up, managing growth, and making tough calls—you gain a level of insight that sharpens the legal guidance you deliver for your clients. When serving a client, there is nothing more powerful than being able to see things from their perspective because you've been there.

I often tell clients, "It's great that you're talking to other attorneys. But ask them—have they ever started a business? Do they actually know what it's like to be in your shoes?" That question doesn't get asked enough in our profession, but it should.

The truth is, you can't offer high-level, sophisticated advice without having lived that experience. Just going through the process of building something real—from scratch—fundamentally changes your perspective. It deepens your understanding and enhances the value of the legal strategy you bring to the table.

At Holt Law, we've been where our clients are. We want to differentiate ourselves from the competition—so our clients can do the same.

And just to rock the boat here, partners at law firms—though they are technically owners—usually don't build the firm from scratch. I've built businesses from nothing, from an idea all the way to six- and seven-figure businesses. That takes energy, time, and methodical work.

The skills you gain from doing this are not the same as those you get from graduating from law school, being an associate at a law firm, and gradually, methodically buying into a firm. That's not running a business. That's buying into something that was already there.

This kind of business acumen is especially helpful when we're preparing a business for sale. We clean everything up. We identify the legal risks, acknowledge them, and bring them out in due diligence. We make sure nothing is being hidden—because hiding something could be fraud. That could have major financial consequences.

As the attorney, I will always advise that we disclose things when we learn them. Lawyers are not allowed to perpetuate fraud. That's easy. But beyond that, as a matter of personal lawyering style, I always advocate for disclosure. If I feel that a client is heading toward something unethical, I have the discretion—and the obligation—to walk away.

And I have done that. I will happily give a refund to avoid shady business transactions.

When I'm involved in a sale—whether I'm the buyer, the seller, or representing either side—I like to have a transition plan that includes the previous owner and keeps them involved for a period of time. We will even put a contingency on money going to that owner based on performance.

Here's an example: Let's say we're buying David's medical practice. The business is doing well, but I want David to stay for a year. I want to pay a portion of the purchase price at the end of that year, contingent on various benchmarks being met.

We do this to make sure the owner sticks around to assure that the marketing, business relationships, and other key factors, are solid. We don't want someone overinflating the value, taking a big purchase price, and disappearing. I like this because it's a collaborative model, but not everyone is open to it. Many people just want to get out. They've already done the preparation, and they want to walk away. But this approach acts as an insurance policy.

If we find a skeleton in the closet during that year—something that wasn't disclosed and isn't covered in the documents—we still have David sitting in his office helping with the transition. We get to look him in the eye, and we confront the problem directly. When you have a transition plan that includes the seller, disclosure is more likely.

Most sellers want the transition period to be short, with as little money as possible tied to future performance. That's completely understandable—they're ready to move on and want to secure their payout. But when I represent the buyer, I usually want the opposite: a longer, more structured transition.

This gives the buyer time to learn the business and builds flexibility to protect their investment. If the seller turns out to be difficult, we can shorten the timeline and shift more of the payment to the back end. Tying a significant amount of the sale price to the seller's continued presence and performance is a smart insurance strategy. It pays dividends in the long run.

This is where strategic deal structure really matters. The time value of money comes into play—because unless interest is added, a payment made a year or two down the road is worth less in real terms than one made up front. That might sound like a small detail, but it can make or break a deal.

Little things like that add up. You have to take advantage of every opportunity available to you. This is what gets me up in the morning—helping people do just that.

You don't have to do it all yourself. And most of the time, it's not worth it. Holt Law exists to make "DIY legal" a thing of the past for health care businesses.

Most people don't think about these details. But we do. That's our role: thinking several steps ahead so our clients don't have to. Holt Law is here to provide real legal strategy—not just counsel during a transaction.

How Can I Help You?

We are a law firm built for health care businesses. As of this writing, we are licensed in Minnesota and California, and we also advise on federal law. We've built strategic connections across the US because health care business law is a highly specialized niche.

I'm selective about who I work with—and that benefits you. Even if I can't serve you directly, I may still be able to connect you to someone I trust.

If your concern involves Minnesota, California, or federal law, we can help you with business transactional matters in health care. We are here to guide and support you as your business grows.

We don't practice criminal law. We don't handle family law or bankruptcies. We do one thing: business law for health care providers and professionals. This includes everything from launching a business to growing, purchasing, or later, selling the business. We deal with the entire life cycle of the business.

That could mean filing the entity, establishing internal policies and procedures, drafting intake paperwork, hiring staff, and navigating contractor versus employee classifications. It could also mean protecting your assets, preparing them for sale, and moving on to your next chapter. We do these things every day. It's our practice.

That's what's unique about me and the firm I've built. I started as a solo practitioner right out of law school. I filed the paperwork and opened up practically the day I was licensed. I haven't looked back.

We operate in a specific, narrow practice area. I work like a surgeon—one who does only one type of procedure—and I do it very well. I chose that procedure because I believe it will have a positive impact on the US health care system.

Helping health care business owners succeed is how I contribute to making the system better.

Unlike many other attorneys, I actually think the companies I work with—like you, the reader—are the ones making a positive impact on the US health care system. When I'm working with you, I feel like I'm on the right side of the fight. You are the hero, and I'm here to help you win.

Not all attorneys can say that. Ask one why they became an attorney and you'll hear all sorts of answers. It's almost like a depressing dinner party. That's not me. I'm highly motivated by the work I do, and I'll continue to do it as long as I can.

I say no to a lot of things because I want to focus on only areas where I'm an expert. I want to be the architect of my law firm and my life. I'm not a generalist. I didn't choose this work because it was an expensive practice area advertised in law school. I chose it because I believe in the clients I serve.

Our positive reviews speak for themselves. I am obsessed with adding value to your life and business. I don't know of any other attorney with such a unique value proposition.

In addition to all that, I've built and run my own successful business. Holt Law is a seven-figure firm with a solid staff beneath it.

Like you, I'm an entrepreneur. I don't just practice law. I own real estate and run an e-commerce business. I don't just speak law—I speak business. I think like an entrepreneur because I am one.

We are pushing the practice of law into the future. I leverage artificial intelligence tools to run a modern, innovative business. Not all attorneys do that.

I am one of the few attorneys in the nation using a refundable flat-fee subscription model. It's designed to deliver value and make legal guidance more accessible. This is all in the service of the health care entrepreneur.

I don't focus on how much I can throw into a retainer or charge for services that may or may not be done. That doesn't help health care businesses grow.

I think that's one of the reasons why I've been successful at a relatively young age. I don't come from a family of attorneys. I'm a first-generation attorney—and that's a good thing. I don't think like a nineteenth-century lawyer who bills by the hour. I think like an entrepreneur. I have an engineering mindset I garnered from my undergrad degree in biomedical engineering.

When I look around at my competitors, I believe you're getting a unicorn of an attorney. I always compete on value, not price. I want you to get as much as you can from our relationship.

You don't see many attorneys offering flat-fee pricing on their website or talking about the things I talk about. But I believe we're entering a new era in the practice of law. And I want to partner with others who share that entrepreneurial mindset.

If this message doesn't resonate with you, I'm probably not the right attorney for you—and that's okay. But if you're reading this book, chances are you have a similar vision.

We are highly selective. That goes both ways. We only serve a highly specialized niche practice area. I'm looking for health care business owners who are navigating the legal landscape of this industry—and want to do it the right way.

If that's who you are, let's move forward together.

Conclusion
Getting Guidance Today

Free Guide and Resources

If you follow me on any social media, you've likely heard me say this: Our blog is an insightful legal resource. You can find it at https://djholtlaw.com/blog/. Other attorneys, and now even AI tools, often pull directly from our blog when answering tough questions. That signals how they regard us as an authoritative source.

Other attorneys reference our blog when giving legal advice to their own clients, which is a testament to our expertise.

We have a variety of free resources on all our social media channels and on our website. If you visit our website and select your specific practice area, you may find downloadable tools specific to your needs. We also answer questions on our YouTube channel. And yes, our consultations are free. It may not necessarily be with an attorney, but it could be, depending on the matter. In any case, we're here for you.

If you're an entrepreneur looking to make a positive impact on the US health care system, then we are the law firm for you. You'll resonate with what we do and how we do it.

The health care system needs more entrepreneurs like you, making a positive impact. I'd be honored to help you do just that.

David					J.					Holt
Holt Law

About the Author

David Holt is the founder and CEO of **Holt Law,** a Minnesota- and California-licensed firm that helps health care entrepreneurs navigate their industry's unique legal challenges.

Drawing on extensive experience in advising health care professionals, medical spa owners, and group home operators, David focuses on regulatory frameworks and **liability protection for group homes and licensed residential care settings**. His expertise enables clients to grow their businesses with confidence and sustainability.

Beyond his legal practice, David is the founder and CEO of DocuHealth, a platform that makes essential legal documents and training accessible to health care professionals.

When he isn't practicing law, David can be found traveling, cold plunging, working out, speaking, hosting his firm's podcast and weekly educational show, and advocating for improvements at the intersection of health care and legal compliance.

Learn more about David's work and Holt Law at djholtlaw.com.

Made in the USA
Coppell, TX
18 January 2026

67761587R00052